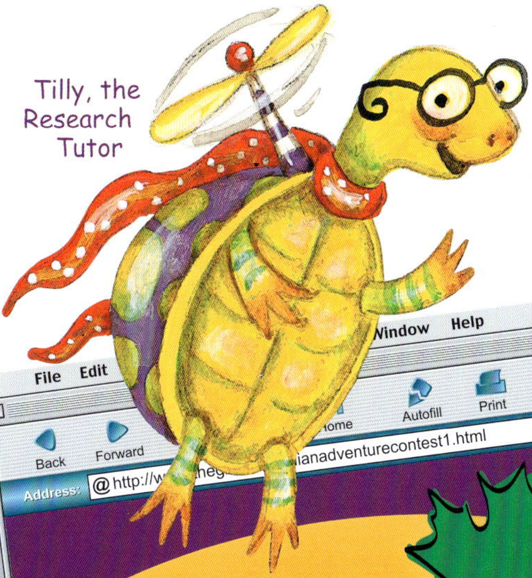

Tilly, the Research Tutor

Do questions 1 to
Tools for Learn

File Edit Window Help

Back Forward Home Autofill Print Mail

Address: @http://w...heg...ianadventurecontest1.html

français | help | search | about us | log out

The Great Canadian Adventure® Contest

Attention all elementary students!

- contest details
- winners and prizes
- for teachers
- for students
- for parents
- how to enter

Win this!

The Contest

"We will be learning about Canada's provinces and territories in social studies class this year," said Ms. Rose. "I have just seen some information about a contest you may want to enter. The contest will help you learn about Canada."

"Cool!" said Alan. "I'm going to enter!"

"Slow down," interrupted Ms. Rose. "Before you enter the contest, we should find out more information. Let's see what the rest of the website says."

File Edit View Go Favorites Tools Window Help

Back Forward Stop Refresh Home Autofill Print Mail

Address: @ http://www.thegreatcanadianadventurecontest1.html

The Great Canadian Adventure® Contest

français | help | search | about us | log

contest details

nners and prizes

for teachers

for students

for parents

how to enter

Do a project on Canada. Your project should

- explain where Canada is located
- include special symbols and information about the government
- show why Canada is a special place to live
- describe the land
- describe the people of Canada

Doing Research

"When do we get started?" asked Alan.

"Well," answered Ms. Rose, "before you start on The Great Canadian Adventure Contest, I need to teach you how to do research. When I use the word *research*, I mean following certain steps to find information on a subject.

"In doing research you should follow the three steps I've listed on the white board. We will be doing most of our research in the library. Tilly who works in the library will help you with your research," concluded Ms. Rose.

Researchers use the following three steps to find information on a subject.

Research 1-2-3®

Research Step 1

Gathering Information®

- Change the research topics into *questions.*
- Start thinking about what type of project you want to work on.
- *Look* for and *make notes* on the best information.

Research Step 2

Looking at and Organizing Information®

- *Read, highlight,* and *organize* your research notes.

Research Step 3

Passing on Information®

- *Pick* a project and *make plans* on when and how to complete it.
- *Prepare* your project.
- *Share* your project.
- *Judge* your project.

Research Step 1 Gathering Information®

Ms. Rose entered the library. The students saw something floating just above her.

"Class," began Ms. Rose, "I would like you to meet Tilly."

"Hi!" said Tilly. "I'm here to help you with The Great Canadian Adventure Contest."

As the students looked on, Tilly flew around the room. Everyone was quiet, which was unusual. Emma giggled and Tina jumped as Tilly landed on the table they were sitting at.

"Neat trick, Ms. Rose," remarked Josh. "You've got the remote control, right?"

Ms. Rose just smiled and continued with the lesson. "Yesterday, we were talking about research. Remember, when we do research we are following three steps to find information on a subject. Tilly is going to teach you how to do this."

Tilly began. "Ms. Rose introduced you to the three steps for doing research. I'm going to give you more information about each step."

Change Research Topics into Questions

Tilly continued. "Let's start with Step 1, Gathering Information. Reread the research topics on the contest's web page (page 3). After you have done this, read the questions on the chart below. Notice that I've changed the research topics from page 3 into questions."

1. Work with a partner.
   a) Turn to page 3 and reread the research topics.
   b) Read the research questions on this page.
   c) Talk about the following:
      How are the research topics and the research questions different? How are they the same? Which ones are easier to work with: the topics or the questions? Tell why.

We want to find out the following:

1. Where is Canada located (found)?
2. What kind of government does Canada have? Describe it. What symbols does Canada have (e.g., flag, national anthem)?
3. What are some special things about Canada? Why is it a special place to live?
4. What does the land look like?
5. What are the people of Canada like? Where do they live? What do they do for a living?
6. (You may want to add some questions of your own.)

Start Gathering Information

Tilly explained. "Most of the information we will need for this project is in the library. We'll be using books, globes, atlases, and computers to do our research.

"Let's start with books. Most of you have been reading storybooks (also called *fiction*). The books you will be using for your project are different from storybooks. They are called *non-fiction* and *reference* books. Non-fiction books and reference books contain information (facts) rather than stories.

"Sarah is sitting on a pile of non-fiction and reference books. She's holding a textbook on Canada and sitting on an encyclopedia, an atlas, an almanac, and a dictionary. Let's talk about each of these in more detail."

Tools for Learning

Non-fiction and reference books contain facts rather than stories.

Non-fiction
Non-fiction books contain information on one subject. This book has information on Canada. It also has maps, drawings, and photographs. These books are a good place to start looking for information.

Almanac
An almanac is a reference book that is made up of facts and records on many subjects. The book *Guinness World Records* is an example of an almanac.

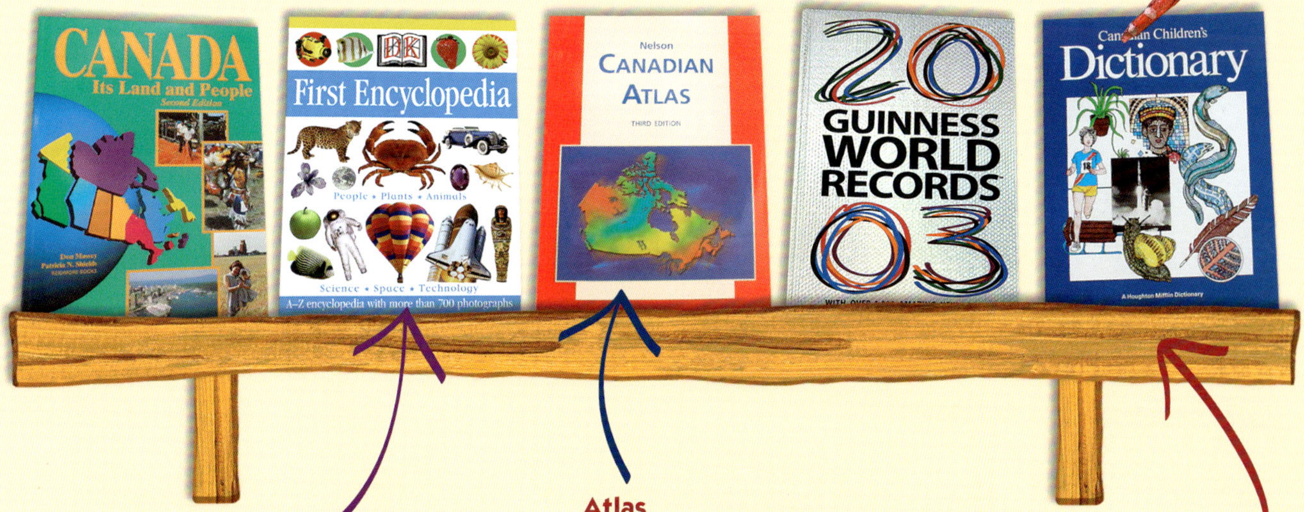

Encyclopedia
An encyclopedia is a reference book or set of books made up of information on many subjects. Encyclopedias have their information in alphabetical order.

Atlas
An atlas is a reference book of maps. Some atlases also have photographs, graphs, and charts.

Dictionary
A dictionary is a reference book that is made up of words and their meanings. The words in a dictionary are in alphabetical order.

"Reference books are a good place to get facts. But there are many other places to find facts. I've listed some of these on the chart," explained Tilly.

- CD-ROMS
- diagrams
- field trips
- globes
- government publications
- graphs and statistics
- internet
- interviews/surveys
- magazines
- maps
- newspapers
- photographs
- speeches
- television programs
- videos

Record the Best Information

Tilly continued her lesson on research. "When you find information that answers the questions you are researching, you should be recording this information. These are called your *research notes*. Do not copy from the book or off the internet. Write the information you find in your own words or make a web with it.

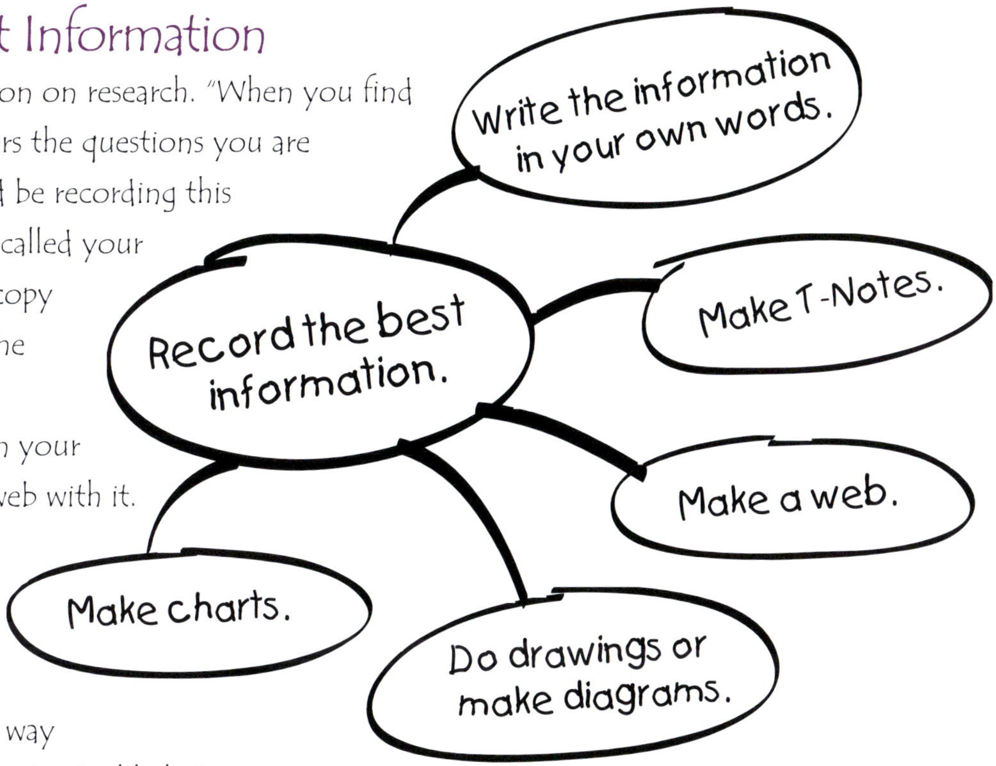

"I'll be joining your group as you look for information on each research question. That way I'll be able to give you individual help."

Research

Step 2

Looking at and Organizing Information®

Tilly appeared in the classroom as the students were working on their research notes.

"I sure have a lot of information," Brandon told Tilly. "It's sort of confusing. What do I do with all this?"

"Well," answered Tilly, "you first need to read through your research notes. Then you should use a felt pen or highlighter pen to colour the most important facts. The facts you highlight should relate to the research question (or topic) you have chosen.

"Next, read the notes you've highlighted. Once you've done this, use only the information you highlighted to make a chart, web, graph, map, or diagram. I'll show you how to do each of these in later classes."

Research Step 3 Passing on Information®

A little later on in the day, Tilly flew into the classroom again. This time she was carrying what appeared to be a heavy suitcase.

"What's in the suitcase, Tilly?" asked Kris.

"Some supplies for doing Research Step 3, Passing on Information. Before I give them to you, let's talk about how you want to share the answers to the research questions. Does anyone have an idea?" asked Tilly.

"We could do a written report," volunteered Emma. "I like to draw so I could add some pictures and a map."

"Or, we could talk about what we find out," suggested Alan.

"I would rather put my information onto a poster, or make a model, or do a multimedia show," offered Josh.

"All excellent ideas," said Tilly. "I suggest you use my **PPSJ**® model. Will everyone look at the chart, so I can explain what **PPSJ**® stands for."

PPSJ® Model

P=Pick a project to share what you've learned. Make plans on when and how you are going to do the project.

P=Prepare your project. Show it to a friend and ask him or her to suggest ways to make it better. Make changes if they are needed.

S=Share your project with your class and your teacher.

J=Judge your project. Record in your journal what you would do differently next time and what you would do the same.

In Conclusion

"Thank you, Tilly, for teaching the class how to do research. Tomorrow, we can start looking for information on the five questions for the contest."

to do

1. Get together with a partner. Either write down or tell each other what five things you have to find out about Canada.
2. Draw a picture in your notes to show the three steps that Tilly gave you to follow when you do research. Write several sentences to explain each step. Check your answers by referring to page 5.
3. Read Tools for Learning 7 (Parts of a Non-fiction Book). Do Task Sheet 2.
4. Do question 5 on Tools for Learning 1 (Previewing).

Glossary

Almanac—a book that is made up of facts and records on many subjects

Atlas—a book of maps

Dictionary—a book made up of words and their meanings

Encyclopedia—a book or a set of books made up of information on many subjects

Government—the people who make the laws and run the country

Graph—a visual way to show information. For example,

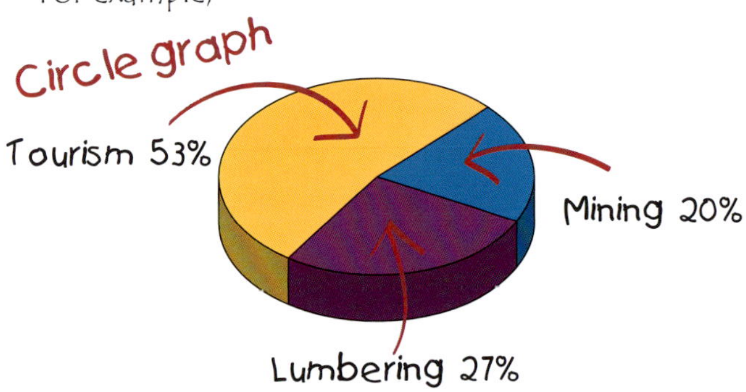

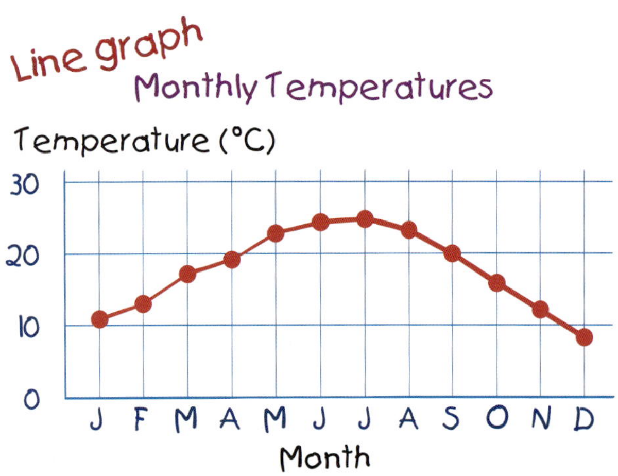

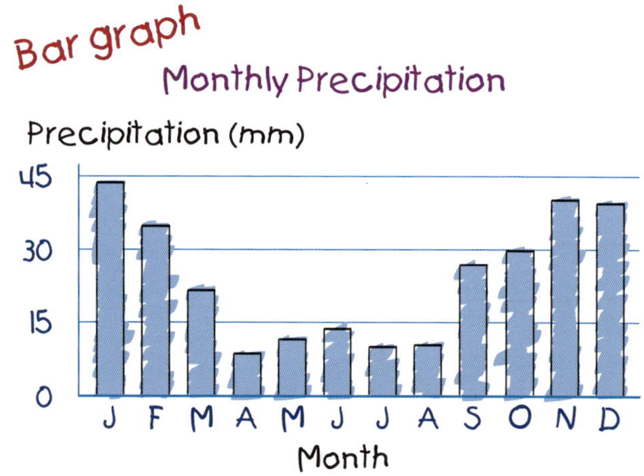

Graphic organizers—charts, webs, graphs, and diagrams to show how ideas are related to each other

Highlight—to underline or colour

Information—facts

Interview—to gather information from a person by asking certain questions

Internet—a network of computers located around the world

Judge—to decide how well a task was done

Multimedia—to share information through words, sound, pictures, and drawings (often done on a computer)

Non-fiction book—a book containing facts rather than stories. Examples include textbooks and books on a variety of subjects.

Project—the finished task, report, or activity

Record—to write down, draw, or put on audiotape or videotape